Technical National Security: The Case of Minuteman Vulnerability and the Soviet Strategic Threat, 1976-1980

Dr. David M. Walsh

TABLE OF CONTENTS.

Introduction.

By the mid-1970s, the Soviet Union had been engaged in a major buildup of its strategic nuclear forces for nearly a decade. The numerical scope of this buildup was impressive—the Soviet strategic arsenal expanded from 1,716 ICBMs and submarine-launched ballistic missiles (SLBM) in 1970 to 2,347 ICBMs and SLBMs in 1977.[i] Additionally, the new family of Soviet ICBMs deployed between 1974 and 1976—the SS-17, SS-18 and SS-19—was capable of carrying multiple, independently-targetable re-entry vehicles (MIRV)[ii] with greater megatonnage and delivering these warheads with greater accuracy than the previous generation of ICBMs. This accuracy-measured in terms of circular error probable (CEP), or the radius of a circle in which half of a missile's warheads are expected to land.[iii]-meant that an area in which the United States heretofore had held an unquestioned lead had been matched by the Soviet Union.

The Case of the Hawks.[iv]

For many American strategic analysts, these developments presented a serious threat to the security of the U.S. nuclear deterrent. During the 1960s, the United States had reorganized its strategic nuclear forces in a Triad posture, consisting of ICBMs, ballistic missile submarines and long-range bombers. The triad concept emphasized redundancy, whereby each of the three "legs," or portions of the triad, would have enough weapons to ensure that the same targets—cities, military installations other industrial centers—would be hit even if the Soviets inflicted considerable damage on one or two legs of the triad. With the improvements in CEP, together with the ability to deliver greater megatonnage (estimated as part of "throw-weight", relating to how much a missile's fuel capacity and motors will allow it to carry), these new missiles appeared to pose a distinct threat to the United States' 1,054 ICBMs, and most particularly to the 550 Minuteman IIIs, the only U.S. ICBMs equipped with MIRV.

The reason these new Soviet ICBMs posed such a threat was due to the basing of ICBMs in concrete silos. These had been effective in the 1960s, when they replaced the earlier mode of deploying ICBMs on vulnerable, above-ground launch pads, which made them dangerously vulnerable to nuclear blasts. Silos, until the mid-1970s, appeared to have solved the problem. Since they were hard to pinpoint and therefore successfully attack, and since their reinforced concrete construction protected the ICBMs from explosions nearby, it was believed that ICBMs were an almost invulnerable strategic asset.

The greater Soviet accuracy, however, meant that this assumption could no longer be taken for granted. The new generation of Soviet ICBMs--particularly the SS-18, which could carry up to eight one-megaton MIRVs and whose modified versions had a CEP of 600 feet[v]--caused considerable alarm in the United States. Among the first to raise the issue of ICBM vulnerability was Paul Nitze. With more than a quarter century of experience, both in and out of government, Nitze was among the most respected U.S. national security analysts. In a January 1976 article published in *Foreign Affairs*, Nitze described his view of the superpower strategic balance, which he saw as shifting

dangerously in favor of the Soviet Union. Criticizing the 1974 Vladivostok Accord, which set the parameters of the SALT II agreement, Nitze described what he saw as the advantages secured by the Soviets and codified by the Accord:

> By 1977, after a Soviet-initiated counterforce strike against the United States to which the United States responded with a counterforce strike, the Soviet Union would have remaining forces sufficient to destroy Chinese and European NATO nuclear capability, attack U.S. population and conventional military targets, and still have a remaining force throw-weight in excess of that of the United States. And after 1977 the Soviet advantage after the assumed attack mounts rapidly.[vi]

In an article published in *Foreign Policy* almost a year later, Nitze reiterated his warnings about the Soviet ICBM threat:

> The Soviet leadership appears to be fully conscious of the differing requirements for countervalue and counterforce capabilities. The question has been asked why the Soviets continue to test high megatonnage single RVs on their SS-18s and SS-19s. I believe that the answer is that they see the importance of deterring the deterrent; in other words, they wish to be able, after a counterforce attack, to maintain sufficient reserve megatonnage to hold U.S. population and industry hostage in a wholly asymmetrical relationship. Concurrently, the accuracy and yield combinations and numbers of MIRVed RVs they are deploying promise to meet their full requirements for a highly effective counterforce capability and still permit the withholding of a substantial number of missiles carrying large single RVs.[vii]

From 1977, the issue of U.S. ICBM vulnerability, as part of an increasing emphasis on growing Soviet military capabilities, began to take shape in the debate about the superpower military balance. The Committee on the Present Danger (CPD), formed in November 1976, criticized the ongoing SALT process in terms of ICBM vulnerability, citing the growing numbers of high-yield Soviet warheads and the related issue of Soviet ICBM throw weight as leading to this situation. In one of its papers, the CPD warned that Soviet ICBM throw weight would measure 11-13 million pounds by the early-1980s, compared to just 3 million for the United States; by that date, it also estimated that the Soviets would have between 6,500 and 9,200 ICBM warheads, compared to just 2,154 American.[viii] For the CPD, this was tantamount to a Soviet nuclear war-winning capability against the United States.

To those who warned of Minuteman vulnerability, the implications were far-reaching. The reasoning of Nitze and others took shape in the following scenario. At some point during the early-1980s, the Soviet Union, confident in its ability to destroy a large percentage (some estimates were as high as 90 per cent) of the U.S. ICBM force, could launch a first strike, using its MIRVed SS-18 and SS-19 ICBMs to deliver a pinpoint attack on U.S. ICBM silos. The Soviets would have a large reserve of ICBMs, together with a large force of ballistic missile submarines at sea and an improved bomber force, centered around the supersonic Backfire, capable of a second strike on U.S. cities. The main concern of the hawks regarded the American response to such an attack. The President of the United States would have only two options: launch an attack on Soviet cities, risking a devastating Soviet strike against U.S. population and infrastructure; or surrender to Soviet demands. Since U.S. submarine-launched ballistic missiles (SLBM)[ix] were not accurate enough to destroy hardened Soviet command, control and communication (C3) centers or ICBM silos, and since the U.S. bomber force faced heavy Soviet air defenses, a countervalue (city-targeting) strike would be the only form of retaliation open to a U.S. President.

It was here that the hawks' main concern lay. The only possible outcome would be either mass devastation and loss of life for the United States in the event of a countervalue strike (Soviet civil defense, it was believed, would ensure considerably lower Soviet casualties in such an exchange) or surrender. The U.S. ICBM force was the only leg of the triad capable of carrying out counterforce missions effectively. Therefore, its destruction or severe attrition would mean that such options would not be available to the United States, and thus mean that the Soviet Union could prevail, in traditional military terms, in the event of a strategic nuclear exchange.

There was also the matter of Soviet strategy in determining weapons development. "Soviet military theorists," wrote Richard Pipes in 1977, "reject the notion that technology (i.e. weapons) decides strategy. They perceive the relationship to be the reverse: strategic objectives determine the procurement and application of weapons." According to Pipes, Soviet strategists believed that "nuclear weapons, coupled with intercontinental missiles, can by themselves carry out strategic missions which previously were accomplished only by means of prolonged tactical operations."[x]

Indeed, Nitze and Pipes, along with other strategic theorists, had made this point in an official capacity. In May 1976, CIA Director George H.W. Bush had authorized an alternative study of the annual CIA estimate of Soviet strategic capabilities.[xi] The group responsible for this study, known as "Team B," included Nitze and Pipes. Its report warned that "The full sweep of these [Soviet strategic] programs, and in particular the great ICBM throw-weight, the improvement and multiplication of MIRVed warheads given that throw-weight and the steady modernization of the ICBM force—e.g. in accuracy and systems reliability—support a conclusion that the Soviets seek clear superiority in the capabilities of these forces, including the maximum feasible counterforce and warfighting capability."[xii]

The authors went on to warn that "The threat includes the steady development of a potential war-winning capability but also encompasses—and reflects—a broader Soviet drive for strategic superiority...The political implications of these strategic capabilities and their role in the overall "correlation of forces"—which we would emphasize—have been insufficiently recognized in past NIEs (National Intelligence Estimates)."[xiii] This report remained classified throughout this time (it was not declassified until 1992), but the concerns about ICBM vulnerability can be seen in its authors' subsequent public writings.

In late 1977, the issue of improved Soviet ICBM accuracy—and counterforce capabilities—came to the fore. In October and November, U.S. satellites recorded six tests of SS-18 and SS-19 missiles. The results of the tests were alarming. The CIA discovered that the a new post-boost vehicle (in which the MIRVs are located) had been added. This included new accelerometers, improved aerodynamic stability for warheads and better timing of warhead release.[xiv] This gave these missiles a CEP of approximately 600 feet.[xv]

This led some analysts to argue for a different view of the strategic balance, and for a shift in American assumptions of what role should be assigned to strategic forces. Among the most forceful of these analysts was Colin S. Gray, who served as assistant director of the International Institute for Strategic Studies (IISS) and at the Hudson Institute during this period. In a 1978 article, Gray made a firm point regarding strategic superiority. "Strategic superiority translates into the ability to control a process of deliberate escalation in pursuit of acceptable terms for war termination."[xvi] For Gray, Nitze and other adherents to this school of thought, the Soviet Union's achievement of such superiority, in Gray's terms, would enable it to decide the shape of a future global conflict.

Gray made a strong case for why the ICBM was a vital leg of the U.S. strategic triad: "The basic case in favor of a strategic forces triad, which includes a substantial and survivable ICBM element, is that it compels a dispersion of adversary investment, preparation and attention."[xvii] If one of the legs of the triad were to be withdrawn, proponents of ICBMs argued, it would be easier for the Soviets to concentrate on the other two legs with improved technological effort. A breakthrough in Soviet anti-submarine warfare (ASW) would render the U.S. ballistic missile submarine force vulnerable. The same would be true of radical improvements in Soviet air defenses *vis a vis* the U.S. bomber force. Either way, the deterrent value of any leg of the triad, if so threatened, would become questionable. The perception of U.S. strategic vulnerability, it was argued, would lead to increased Soviet boldness in undertaking geopolitical advances in Africa, the Middle East and even Europe. Only a strong, credible U.S. deterrent would maintain stability and eliminate the risk of Soviet adventurism. As Gray wrote:

> "In political terms, which is the proper way to view the strategic arms competition, the ultimate point is that the United States cannot tolerate Soviet unilateral acquisition of a near-total silo-threatening capability, or being coerced into a strategic forces dyad [submarines and bombers only] (with the attendant simplification of Soviet defensive tasks)."[xviii]

This was a counter to the doves' views (discussed below) about the supposed obsolescence of the ICBM and the ability of ballistic missile submarines and bombers to maintain deterrence independently from ICBMs. In other words, Gray, Nitze, Pipes and other hawks saw the debate in geopolitical and strategic terms, whereas the doves tended to view it strictly in terms of absolute military capacity.

The best response to the vulnerability of silo-based ICBMs, for these analysts, was the development and deployment of mobile ICBMs, most notably the MX. This missile, under advanced development since 1974,[xix] would give the United States the ability to carry out counterforce strikes against hardened Soviet targets in a secure configuration, thus upsetting Soviet attempts to gain strategic superiority and any attendant geopolitical benefits. As Gray wrote in 1981, "Its [the MX] very existence should be a nightmare for Soviet defense planners. They cannot ignore such a potent U.S. capability—yet they cannot attack it in expectation of net gain."[xx] The ICBM, with its secure communication links (ground-based, as opposed to the more difficult tasks of communications with submarines and bombers), its prompt hard-target kill potential (ability to strike hardened military targets in under half-an-hour) and accuracy (including the ability to strike ICBM silos, which MIRVed Minuteman IIIs had by the late-1970s), would therefore be vital in maintaining a credible U.S. strategic deterrent in the face of Soviet strategy and technological advances.

The Case of the Doves.

For many defense analysts, the Soviet threat to U.S. ICBMs, while real, did not require the response that conservatives called for, namely a new mobile ICBM. The Center for Defense Information (CDI), a liberal defense analysis center in Washington, D.C., devoted several issues of its monthly publication, the *Defense Monitor*, to an analysis of ICBM vulnerability and the issues surrounding MX deployment. In the March 1978 issue, George Kistiakowsky, who had served as President Eisenhower's assistant for science and technology, argued that the fears of Nitze, Gray and others regarding a disarming Soviet first strike were unfounded. In analyzing out the difficulty the Soviets would have in coordinating such a strike, Kistiakowsky cited the phenomenon of fratricide, in which exploding warheads would destroy other incoming warheads close behind, meaning that some targeted silos would not be destroyed, allowing for the defender to retaliate with surviving ICBMs. Furthermore, fratricide would impede a Soviet attack "in ways and for periods of time that cannot be calculated accurately in advance."[xxi] Kistiakowsky also cited an important factor—warning time—as being an inhibiting factor to the Soviets:

"Nor would it be a simple matter for the Soviets to catch us off our guard with a surprise attack. We would in all likelihood have advance warnings of less obvious nature than the trek of millions of Muscovites armed with shovels to the countryside. [alluding to urban evacuation, the key element in Soviet civil defense plans] Our space sensors would be primed to signal a Soviet launch; or they would be put out of commission in advance by Soviet antisatellite systems, and this in itself would alert us to imminent attack. The Soviets well know that, instead of waiting a minute longer, the American President could order our own ICBM's launched against the Soviet Union, leaving empty silos for the Soviets to destroy."[xxii]

Elaborating on these issues, Andrew Cockburn pointed out another difficulty, that of ensuring that all the systems—the rockets at various stages, the navigation and geodesy equipment, and the warheads' arming fuses—would work perfectly at the precise times, from launch to detonation on target, in order to succeed in destroying a Minuteman in its silo.[xxiii] This, of course, is the process for just *one* missile. As Cockburn went on to explain, "a first strike requires that all these processes, from first-stage ignition to the final explosion, be repeated hundreds of thousands of times in an operation for which there can be no full-scale rehearsal and no second chance."[xxiv]

Where doves and hawks disagreed most, however, was over the issue of secure second-strike forces. The CDI, in its March 1978 publication, went to great lengths to describe just how effective these forces were in deterring a Soviet first strike. The U.S. bomber force, consisting of B-52 and FB-111 aircraft, had a 30 per cent alert rate, meaning that 120 bombers, as well as supporting tanker aircraft, could be airborne in five minutes. The CDI estimated that about 85 per cent of these aircraft could reach their targets. Furthermore, about 28 of the U.S. Navy's 41 ballistic missile submarines were normally deployed at sea, carrying 3,600 warheads. These forces would be more than enough to devastate the Soviet Union in the event of a first strike on the Minuteman and Titan silos.[xxv] Addressing the question of perceptions regarding ICBM vulnerability, the authors pointed out that

> "The Soviets understand that a nuclear weapon delivered by a bomber or a submarine-launched missile explodes in the same way as one delivered by an ICBM. Either our retaliatory forces can inflict enough damage to make nuclear war unthinkable for Soviet leaders or they cannot: the mode of delivery is secondary. If some people do not grasp this fact, then the answer is to provide them with better information, not to construct costly new forces for the sake of appearances."[xxvi]

Whereas the hawks viewed *perceived* capabilities as being of importance in the strategic balance, the doves saw *actual* capabilities as the measure of strategic deterrence, and thus the element that would maintain it.

This was not just the view of private defense experts, but also of some who had been involved in the SALT negotiations. Jan Lodal, who had been a member of the National Security Council and had been present at Vladivostok, argued that "even if The Soviets destroyed all our land-based ICBMs, non-alert bombers and non-alert submarine-launched ballistic missiles (SLBMs), we would still retain our alert bomber force and our alert SLBM force. These forces alone would be capable of delivering something like 4-5,000 nuclear weapons against Soviet targets."[xxvii] Cockburn pointed out that "just two of the comparatively old-fashioned Poseidon [SLBM] submarines would demolish 200 Soviet cities."[xxviii] Christopher Coker, writing in 1983 about U.S. defense issues in the 1970s, went further. Citing official U.S. sources, Coker described the vulnerability of the Soviet economy to a relatively small number of U.S. strategic warheads:

> "So concentrated is Soviet industry that the Office of Technology Assessment believes that only three Minuteman III ICBMs and seven Poseidon SLBMs could devastate nearly 75 per cent of Soviet industrial refining capacity. The Arms Control and Disarmament Agency also believes that a mere six Poseidon SLBMs, with their 54 warheads, the ultimate counter-value weapon, could destroy 150 plants which produce 50 per cent of Russia's primary metals, petroleum, chemicals, synthetic rubber and power generators."[xxix]

The issue of Soviet ICBM accuracy was also questioned by skeptics of American vulnerability. Lodal argued that while Soviet ICBMs would, in theory have an 85 per cent chance of destroying U.S. silos, "this is no better than the effectiveness expected from the

Minuteman III once the improved Mark 12A warhead is deployed and certain low-cost accuracy improvements are made. Yet, it would take at last three times as much throw-weight for the Soviets to deploy these 1.5 megaton warheads as it would for the United States to deploy the Mark 12A."[xxx] Even after the SS-18 and SS-19 tests of 1977, the SS-18 Mod (Model) 2, the upgraded variant of this missile, and the SS-19 had a CEP of 0.25 nautical miles (nm.), while the Minuteman III, even without the Mark 12A, had a CEP of 0.2nm. The Minuteman II, with a single one-megaton warhead, had a CEP of 0.3nm., equal to the original SS-18 and SS-17.[xxxi] It is important to note that the Mark 12A was considered to give the Minuteman III a true anti-silo capability, above and beyond what the original Mark 12, whose characteristics are listed above, could attain.

For some, the vulnerability of U.S. ICBMs, projected for the early and mid-1980s, was seen as an opportunity to reduce nuclear arsenals. The CDI advocated the withdrawal of these as a means of reducing Soviet strategic alert levels, stabilizing the arms race, shifting from a counterforce strategy, and reduce excess defense spending.[xxxii] It also argued against deployment of the MX on grounds of cost, strategic instability (its accuracy as a counterforce weapon and the difficulties of verification in SALT II), and technical feasibility (the various schemes might not be practical.)[xxxiii] These considerations were influenced by the view that the United States already had enough submarine- and bomber-launched weapons to do ensure deterrence. Such thinking reflected the core view of the doves on this subject: that U.S. strategic forces were more than capable of deterring their Soviet counterparts, regardless of the threat posed to U.S.

ICBMs.

The Official View.

The Secretaries of Defense.

Donald Rumsfeld became Secretary of Defense in October 1975, a few months before Paul Nitze would make his fears of ICBM vulnerability public with his article in *Foreign Affairs*. As this issue grew in importance from 1976, Rumsfeld increasingly stressed Soviet counter-silo capabilities and the threat posed by the new ICBMs. In his Fiscal Year (FY) 1977 report, Rumsfeld stated that three of four Soviet ICBMs, the SS-17, -18, and -19, had been deployed. This fact, along with other developments during 1975-76, presented a threat to the U.S. ICBM force. As Rumsfeld wrote:

> "The probability of kill against hard targets such as ICBM silos is most sensitive to missile accuracy. It is this feature of the new Soviet ICBM program which, with multiple high-yield warheads, translates into a potential hard target capability, unmatched by the U.S. As the Soviets proceed with their expected ICBM deployment and continued improvements in accuracy, the combination of increased throw-weight, MIRVing and improving accuracy will increasingly threaten the survivability of our fixed-silo Minuteman force."[xxxiv]

Rumsfeld reiterated this warning in his FY 1978 report. "Before the mid-1980s, the Soviets could possibly have the capability, with a small fraction of their ICBMs, to destroy the bulk of the Minuteman/Titan force."[xxxv]

On the same page of the report, a graph, depicting U.S. ICBM silo survivability in relation to Soviet capabilities, showed descending lines from 1976 to 1985. This was an indication that, due to improvements in Soviet throw weight, accuracy and warhead yield, the survival of U.S. ICBMs was in increasing jeopardy.

It is interesting to note that by this time (January 1977), the "Team B" report had already been published, and Paul Nitze had been publicly warning of the dangers posed by improved Soviet strategic forces, particularly ICBMs, for nearly a year. The last sentence indicates an approach that the U.S. defense establishment had been considering for the past few years, a mobile ICBM. Still, it reflected Rumsfeld's view that the Soviet Union did not have the ability to eliminate with confidence the U.S. strategic forces, which included ballistic missile submarines and bombers. This implied a different view on the part of the Pentagon than that expressed by those like Nitze and Pipes who had formulated the "Team B" report.

Nor was the Soviet Union ahead, in Rumsfeld's estimation, in the accuracy of its strategic missiles. In another report from 1977, in a table titled "Strategic Forces Balance," hard-target destruction potential (the ability to destroy hardened enemy military installations like C3 centers and missile silos) was listed in the column showing U.S. leads, as opposed to those of the USSR.[xxxvi] Rumsfeld's concern was with future developments, which were shaped by current trends, and on the effects these could have on American options at the level of strategic nuclear conflict. "A continuation of Soviet strategic programs—even within the constraints of SALT—could threaten the survivability of the Minuteman force within a decade. If that should be allowed to happen, our ability to respond to less than full-scale attacks in a controlled and deliberate fashion would be severely curtailed, and strategic stability could be endangered."[xxxvii] This, combined with the aging of the other elements of the triad (Polaris submarines and B-52 bombers) and the continuation of vigorous Soviet strategic force modernization, meant, in Rumsfeld's view, that a danger existed whereby "the Soviet strategic capability will come to be seen as superior to that of the United States."[xxxviii]

Harold Brown, Rumsfeld's successor as Defense Secretary, took a more cautious view of Minuteman vulnerability. In his first report to Congress, in 1978, Brown described the problem in detail, and also put it into the perspective of the overall strategic balance:

"The potential vulnerability of our existing silo-based ICBM force (MINUTEMAN and TITAN II) is a major issue of concern to us, but it is important that the issue be approached in perspective. Because ICBM silos are fixed and known targets, we have recognized for years that once Soviet accuracy improved enough, the silos would become vulnerable.

"It is now clear that all three of the 'fourth generation' ICBMs the Soviets are now deploying—the SS-17, SS-18, and SS-19—have the potential, with feasible accuracy improvements, to attain high single-shot kill probabilities against U.S. silos. A relatively small fraction of the current generation Soviet MIRVed ICBMs could, by the early-to-mid-1980s, reduce the number of surviving MINUTEMAN to low levels."[xxxix]

Brown went on to describe the dangers inherent for the Soviet Union in attempting to launch a counterforce attack on the Minuteman force:

"Even if such an attack worked exactly as predicted, the Soviets would face great risks and uncertainties. First, they would necessarily have to consider whether the U.S. missiles would still be in their silos when the attack arrived, or whether, given our capability to have unambiguous confirmation of a massive attack, we would launch from under the attack. Second, and more important, an attack intended to destroy U.S. silos could kill at least several million Americans and would leave untouched at least the alert bombers and at-sea SSBNs with thousands of warheads. The Soviets might—and should—fear that, in response, we would retaliate with a massive attack on Soviet cities and industry."[xl]

"In short," Brown summarized, "the vulnerability of MINUTEMAN is a problem, but even if we did nothing about it, it would not be synonymous with the vulnerability of the United States, or even of the strategic deterrent."[xli]

By 1979, the position of the hawks on this issue, disseminated to a considerable degree by groups like the CPD, had become a major focus of debate on the strategic balance. Accordingly, in his report for FY 1980, Brown did stress the need for ICBM vulnerability to be reduced. "We must take the prospective vulnerability of our ICBM force with the utmost seriousness for planning purposes," the report stated. "A focus of our planning, in these circumstances, is on how to deal with this problem. SALT II will leave open all options."[xlii] As far as a stable strategic balance was concerned, however, Brown was confident. "In my judgement, we currently have an adequate strategic deterrent...I believe, moreover, that we can maintain the deterrent for the foreseeable future with the resources we have requested in the FY 1980 defense budget, and in the Long-Range Defense Projection we have developed (into the mid-1980s)."[xliii]

During 1979, development of the MX mobile ICBM continued. Studies of possible launch modes and configurations were undertaken. Furthermore, SALT II, signed in June 1979, allowed for its development. As opposed to the more general statements in his earlier reports, Brown, in his 1981 report, took a much more direct approach in describing what was being—and would be—done to rectify Minuteman vulnerability. "Reducing the vulnerability of the land-based ICBM force is the highest priority strategic initiative in the five-year program."[xliv] Brown also described just why the MX was necessary. "The decision to proceed with full-scale development of the MX reflects the Administration's view that there are persuasive military and perceptual reasons for increasing the deterrent value of the ICBM component of our strategic forces."[xlv] In his last report to Congress in 1981, Brown described possible interim efforts to reduce vulnerability, like deployment of MX in Minuteman silos or, conversely, the deployment of Minuteman in a multiple point system (MPS).[xlvi] Such an emphasis on rectifying ICBM vulnerability reflected both strategic and political considerations on the part of the Carter Administration.

The improved accuracy of Soviet ICBMs, particularly from 1977, had, no doubt, played a role in shaping Harold Brown's perceptions of Minuteman vulnerability. However, the political situation cannot be ignored either. The rising tide of voices from groups like the CPD, criticizing SALT II as undermining American security, meant that development of the mobile, survivable MX missile became a necessity for the Carter Administration. With the mood in Congress swinging toward funding of MX research and development, Brown, while emphasizing the essential stability of the strategic relationship, increasingly took the position of the perception of weakness in discussing the issue. This meant that, to some extent, he had to display to legislators what was being done by the Pentagon to surmount the difficulties presented by this issue. As the problem of potential U.S. ICBM vulnerability grew, so did Brown's efforts to find a possible remedy.

The Military View.

The view of the U.S. Armed Forces played a considerable role in influencing opinion on both defense spending and arms control, due to their first hand professional knowledge of the subject. The position of the U.S. military's top officers was that the maintenance of a triad of forces was of vital importance to the security of the United

States and to strategic stability. In March 1977, Lt. General Alton D. Slay, USAF, testified before the Senate Armed Services Committee on the need for the triad to be maintained:

"We are, as you know, deeply imbedded in the Triad with all of our strategic weapons. We feel the synergistic effect of one to the other is extremely important...We complicate the enemy's attack problem. If he can attack our ICBM force, he will hesitate if he cannot accurately determine whether or not he can do away with our submarines and with our bombers. The Triad also provides a hedge against any technological breakthrough which the enemy might have in countering any of our Triad weapons."[xlvii]

Slay pointed out the importance of ICBMs to the triad. "Contribution to the Triad—in terms of nuclear delivery vehicles—ICBMs compose better than half." An accompanying pie chart showed that ICBMs contributed 52 per cent of nuclear delivery vehicles, 23 per cent of weapons (warheads) and 32 per cent of total megatonnage.[xlviii] While lower than the level allotted to ICBMs as part of the Soviet strategic force, this was still considerable.

The Office of the Joint Chiefs of Staff (JCS), the senior military advisory body to the President, was key to disseminating the military position on these matters. The Chairman of the JCS, as key military adviser to the President, was the most important uniformed individual to give such advice. General George S. Brown of the U.S. Air Force served as JCS Chairman from 1974 to 1978. In the *United States Military Posture* statement for 1976, General Brown outlined both the current U.S.-Soviet strategic balance and the future trends affecting that balance:

"The static measures of relative military strength today remain in rough equilibrium. But in a technological era marked by giant strides in both science and engineering, we must approach the future with firmness and caution—firmness in our resolve to stabilize the static balance, and caution in minimizing the chance of technological surprise.

"There is mounting evidence that the Soviet Union is pressing forward vigorously with massive programs for near-term deployments involving every facet of offensive strategic power. At the same time, it is improving appreciably, at a more gradual rate, capabilities for strategic defense and pursuing with firm determination development of advanced technology appropriate to the entire strategic equation.

"The Soviet Union's focus is not simply on maintaining the current advantage in terms of megatonnage and throwweight, but it applies as well to accuracy, flexibility, survivability, and MIRVing intercontinental missiles."[xlix]

While General Brown's report described the spectrum of Soviet strategic weapons development rather than specific Soviet policy (as described in the Pentagon's *Annual Reports*), he did warn of the capabilities of the SS-18, which began to be deployed by the time the report was written (1975). "This missile, with much greater destructive power than Titan [the largest U.S. ICBM] and improved accuracy, is capable of destroying any known fixed target."[l] Limitations on Soviet heavy ICBMs were becoming an issue of ever greater importance for the United States (the Vladivostok Accord limited numbers of heavy ICBM launchers, or silos, to 308 for the Soviet Union), and General Brown's warning, which combined with his view of Soviet strategic modernization and Donald Rumsfeld's concerns, made a strong case for official action regarding the issue of ICBM vulnerability.

The following year, General Brown was more sanguine about Soviet capabilities. "The Soviets will achieve significant improvements in ICBM accuracy, force survivability, and offensive flexibility, including improved hard target capabilities. The new ICBMs being deployed [i.e. SS-17, SS-18 and SS-19, along with the proposed SS-16 mobile ICBM] are much more accurate than the systems they are replacing. Moreover, these accuracies are expected to improve further as the Soviets continue their test programs and refine and modify selected missile components."[li] In summarizing the strategic balance, General Brown stated "Their [the Soviets'] new programs are clearly designed to provide the Soviet Union with diversified and flexible strategic offensive forces that will improve the Soviet war-fighting posture." A major reason for this, and which pointed to U.S. ICBM vulnerability, was due to "increasing capabilities to strike hard targets."[lii] "With the new generation of MIRVed ICBM's currently being deployed by the Soviet Union, vulnerability of the US silo based ICBM force will increase over the long term."[liii]

General Brown, in concluding his discussion of the strategic balance, suggested ways for the United States to improve the survivability of its ICBM force:

"We may be required within the framework of a subsequent SAL [Strategic Arms Limitation] agreement to develop alternative basing modes for our land-based ICBMs in the event the USSR does develop and deploy that combination of accuracy and yield which would threaten the survivability of MINUTEMAN as currently deployed. We Also must provide an option to increase the number of RVs[re-entry vehicles] and the throwweight of our present systems in the event such action becomes necessary *to preserve the perception of equilibrium which, in the long run, may be as important as equilibrium itself and is essential for stability*"[liv] (My italics).

General Brown's emphasis, as can be seen, was to provide, through a SALT II agreement, the ability for the United States to develop a large mobile ICBM with greater MIRV capability. As he keenly saw, perception, as well as actuality, was a keen indicator of the state of the strategic balance between the superpowers.

As with the Secretaries of Defense during this time General Brown made a strong case for the MX ICBM, calling it "the most significant strategic initiative being proposed."[lv] He continued: "The MX will retain the prompt, high confidence, counterattack capabilities of the existing ICBM force. Additionally, it will ensure maintenance of strategic balance despite projected enhancement of Soviet hard target kill capability."[lvi]

In his last posture statement to Congress the following year, General Brown reiterated his warning about Soviet strategic capabilities and the threat these posed to international stability:

"Continuing Soviet investment in advanced technology in combination with impressive production rates suggest the capability for achieving distinct strategic and operational advantages in technology and rapidly increased force levels—advantages which could offer opportunities for coercion or adventurism at the expense of the United States and its allies."[lvii]

This view echoed that of the CPD regarding Soviet capabilities and the intentions that lay behind them.

As a serving officer, General Brown did have first-hand knowledge of Soviet ICBM improvements, particularly those that had been carried out in November 1977, just two months before this report was issued. He noted in describing Soviet ICBM capability that "ICBM accuracies are expected to improve further as the Soviets continue their test programs and refine and modify selected components. The Soviet hard target kill capability could be somewhat better than previously estimated."[lviii] As this passage indicates, the tests were still in their early stages, but further testing would most certainly refine the capabilities of the new generation Soviet ICBMs, particularly the SS-18 and SS-19, considerably.

General Brown's successor as JCS Chairman was General David C. Jones. Whereas Brown had warned of the growing Soviet threat, Jones took a more strident tone. In describing the strategic balance in his first military posture statement, Jones reiterated Brown's concerns with ICBM vulnerability and emphasized the overall adverse trends in the strategic balance:

> "A critical concern in this area [strategic nuclear forces] is the impending threat to the survivability of our land-based ICBM force, a development which will impose serious strains upon the delicate structure of crisis stability in the early to mid-1980s. However, the broader threats to stability, in my view, are the overall size and asymmetrical momentum of modernization of both sides' strategic arsenals.
>
> "These objectives can be realized only through a balanced strategy of negotiations and programs...Of particular importance is a commitment to a program for a survivable ICBM."[lix]

Jones' view reflected that of the Carter Administration regarding arms control, namely deep reductions in the most capable Soviet offensive weapons like the SS-18. However, he also called for modernization of American capabilities. "I believe that it will be essential to spend more on our strategic forces. The increase need not be as large with an equitable SALT agreement as without, but in either event, we will have to do more in this area."[lx] This was also the view of the CPD and members of Congress, most notably Senator Henry Jackson. Jones also cited the need for deployment of the MX. "Advances in missile accuracy enable them to field ICBMs which are expected, by the early-1980s, to place the US MINUTEMAN force in jeopardy...Increased hardening of ICBM sites will not solve the problem or reduce the vulnerability appreciably."[lxi] Later, Jones reported, "The MX program is the only significant US land-based ICBM initiative being considered. When combined with survivable basing, MX would provide a valuable counterweight to Soviet strategic momentum and a hedge against future uncertainties in the strategic environment"[lxii]

During the year that elapsed between the preparation of the posture statements for 1980 and 1981, a number of developments occurred that weakened and then finished the process of Détente, leading to what is known as the "Second Cold War." The debate over the ratification of SALT II and the Soviet invasion of Afghanistan were the most obvious of these. In his introduction to the 1981 report, General Jones clearly indicated what he saw as the danger of an imbalance of strategic forces:

> "I anticipate such a disparity would be reflected in a more confident Soviet leadership, increasingly inclined toward more adventurous behavior in areas where our interests clash and where US ability to respond by conventional means would be circumscribed. The Soviet invasion of Afghanistan could well be a "leading edge" event reflecting precisely such a heightened confidence. Such a situation carries the seeds of serious miscalculation and runs the risk of precipitating a confrontation which neither side wants nor intends."[lxiii]

In a chart, General Jones indicated that Soviet time-urgent hard target kill potential, or the ability to strike hardened military targets swiftly and thus eliminate them at the start of a counterforce nuclear exchange, had surpassed that of the United States from 1977. Furthermore, the overall hard target kill potential, which remained slightly in the United States' favor, was roughly equal from 1981 through the rest of the decade.[lxiv]

In his final report, for FY 1982, General Jones again emphasized ICBM vulnerability and the consequences of a resulting strategic disparity between the United States and the Soviet Union. "A very serious weapon system concern is the growing vulnerability of our land-based/ICBM force, the key contributor to our time-urgent hard target kill capacity. Without a high degree of survivability afforded by the MX missile system, the deterrence and crisis stability of this most precisely controllable component of our strategic force mix could be seriously compromised."[lxv]

In the first chapter of the report, under the sub-heading "The Dangerous Decade Ahead," this theme was reiterated. "Improved accuracy and MIRVing of Soviet intercontinental ballistic missiles increasingly threaten the survivability of US fixed land-based strategic systems, with dangerous impacts on the overall strategic relationship."[lxvi] So serious was this that Jones, in his section on strategic forces in Chapter II on the military balance, stated that "US capability to avoid coercion and exert leverage in a crisis is eroding in direct relation to continuing Soviet force improvements and the aging of US strategic nuclear systems. This erosion contributes more than any other factor to the danger confronting US interests in the 1980s."[lxvii]

As with the Secretaries of Defense, particularly Harold Brown, the views of the JCS Chairmen reflected the shift in American perceptions of Soviet ICBM capabilities. Whereas the JCS would support SALT II, the need for a survivable U.S. ICBM to counter Soviet developments, particularly from 1977, was also stressed with equal vigor. As U.S.-Soviet relations deteriorated from 1978 onwards, both Generals Brown and Jones emphasized the link between Soviet capabilities and possible intentions, just as had the "Team B" authors and the CPD. For both JCS Chairmen, the remedy would be the MX.

Effects on Policy and U.S.-Soviet Relations.

The Pentagon and the JCS were not alone in viewing the increased vulnerability of U.S. ICBMs during this time. The U.S. Congress began taking a keen interest in the issue. Among its most vocal members was Senator Henry M. Jackson, who had been highly critical of the SALT process on grounds that it had allowed the Soviets to establish an advantage in strategic forces *vis a vis* the United States. In February 1977, Jackson sent a memo to President Carter outlining his views on an equitable SALT II agreement. "In the effort ultimately to reduce our dependence on nuclear weapons," Jackson wrote, "a SALT II agreement should not: Impair our security by increasing the vulnerability of our strategic forces…or the credibility that they would be used if necessary to defend against attack" or "leave the United States vulnerable to the rapid acquisition of a significant Soviet advantage if the agreement is abrogated or violated."[lxviii] Later, in advising against the Soviet SALT proposal regarding ICBMs, Jackson noted that

> "It would do nothing to limit the developing Soviet capability to destroy our own land-based missile force. Even with significant reductions in the ceiling of strategic delivery vehicles such an agreement would fail to alleviate that threat, because it continues a 300 to 54 Soviet advantage in modern 'heavy' missiles and because it acquiesces in the Soviet insistence that their new, large MIRVed SS-19 be defined as a 'light' missile."[lxix]

Jackson later spelled out his own view of how this should be dealt with in the SALT negotiations. "It should be made clear to the Russians that failure to make this (admittedly) substantial change [classifying the SS-19 as a heavy ICBM] could result in U.S. deployment of a "light" M-X of equal if not superior offensive capability."[lxx]

In October 1978, the U.S. House of Representatives' Armed Services Committee issued a report titled "Land-Based ICBM Forces Vulnerability and Options," addressing the issue of ICBM vulnerability. It agreed strongly with what top officials, most notably Donald Rumsfeld and General Jones, had said about this issue. "The possession of a vulnerable strategic weapon system tends to destabilize the strategic balance of power, especially during times of crisis," the report stated. "Hence decisive action by the United States is necessary if the country is to avoid being placed in the position of possessing a vulnerable strategic weapon system."[lxxi] It went on to identify the importance of the deployment of mobile ICBMs as part of the ongoing SALT II process:

"There is an urgent need to understand and address this issue before SALT II is consummated to insure that the United States does not foreclose any of its options to maintain its strategic position, especially in light of massive Soviet strategic improvement programs. This is the central issue in the debate over MX: It transcends issues concerning the details of the MX mission and the size, small or large, or the MX missiles."[lxxii]

In identifying the threat to U.S. ICBMs, the report again linked Soviet technological advances with SALT II:

"Technological improvements being implemented by the Soviet Union, at a rate unprecedented in the history of the strategic arms race, and the proposed SALT II Treaty and Protocol, are the outside issues affecting the survivability of the land based ICBM's and their future role in the strategic balance.

"As the technology becomes available to, and is implemented by, the Soviet Union, the overwhelming throw-weight superiority of Soviet systems…creates a threat to the once invulnerable U.S. ICBM system…The situation is complicated by SALT since the proposed treaty permits the Soviets to exploit this basic advantage."[lxxiii]

After a discussion of the technical aspects of ICBM accuracy, implications for arms control and the possibility of utilizing other weapons, including air-launched cruise missiles for ICBMs, the report concluded that

"The dilemma then is this. *The Means to provide a survivable ICBM require changes in the current thinking on SALT*. The debate over how to reconcile this dilemma should be held *before* the debate on SALT II. Waiting until after SALT II could foreclose many options, some of which may be essential to national security."[lxxiv]

While this was more an description of the issue than an endorsement of a particular policy, the Congress did in fact begin major funding from FY 1978 for the MX. Whereas only $159 million had been spent on the program up to FY 1977, an additional $134 million had been spent by the end of FY 1978. Another $732 million was spent in 1980, bringing the total to $2.45 billion by FY 1981.[lxxv] This indicated that the Congress was increasingly taking the view that a remedy for ICBM vulnerability, namely the MX mobile ICBM, had to be found and implemented.

Where the ICBM vulnerability debate would have the most obvious impact, as far as U.S.-Soviet relations were concerned, was in the drafting of SALT II. The Vladivostok Accords of November 1974, signed by President Ford and Soviet General Secretary Leonid Brezhnev, allowed the USSR to maintain a force of 308 large ICBMs, the SS-18's category. At the time, it was realized that while Soviet heavy ICBMs were an issue in arms control negotiations, even reductions of such weapons would not likely alter the strategic balance markedly in favor of the United States.

The minutes of a National Security Council Meeting on December 22, 1975 reflect this fact. President Ford discussed the issue of strategic forces with such important policymakers as General Brown, Secretary Rumsfeld, Secretary of State Henry Kissinger, and CIA Director William Colby. Addressing the issue of ICBM vulnerability as related to SALT II, Colby noted that:

"There is also the question of the effectiveness of the Soviet strategic forces against hardened targets in the U.S. Soviet progress in this area will depend on the quality of their missiles, *and will be largely independent of SALT TWO*…

"Our best estimate of Soviet offensive force developments over the next ten years, *even under* SALT TWO limitations, is that Soviet ICBM forces will probably pose a major threat to U.S. Minuteman silos in the early 1980s."[lxxvi] (My italics.)

Nonetheless, the Ford Administration did take heed of possible strategic developments that would offset Soviet heavy ICBMs. In the summary of the aide-memoire[lxxvii] issued by Secretary Kissinger on December 10, 1974, the subject of mobile ICBMs was raised. "The prospect of increasing vulnerability of silos to highly accurate MIRVs suggests replacing fixed land-based missiles by land-mobile or air-launched ICBMs."[lxxviii]

Upon taking office in January 1977, the Carter Administration found itself grappling with this issue. In a meeting held on February 1, 1977 with Anatoly Dobrynin, the Soviet ambassador to the United States, Carter, together with Secretary of State Cyrus Vance and National Security Adviser Zbigniew Brzezinski, brought up the issue of Soviet ICBM throw-weight, to which Dobrynin cited U.S. advantages in accuracy as necessitating this Soviet advantage.[lxxix]

The issue of Soviet heavy ICBMs would soon become part of the U.S. negotiating package. The minutes of a meeting of the National Security Council's Special Coordinating Committee (SCC) on February 3, 1977, "Secretary Vance noted that this was an extremely important aspect of our position and that we should not recede from our proposal to limit the number…to 190." However, the minutes continue, "the

Soviets were very strongly resisting this limitation on grounds that the question of limitations on heavy missiles had been agreed in the Vladivostok Accords."[lxxx]

In March 1977, Vance traveled to Moscow to set forth the new administration's arms control agenda. The key element in this was the so-called "Comprehensive Proposal," which would see the Soviet Union reduce its SS-18 force from 308 to 150, significantly below even what Vance had suggested in the SCC meeting a month earlier. For its part, the United States would cancel development and deployment of MX. As David Dunn points out, "this meant an opportunity to swap the MX for s substantial reduction in the Soviet threat to Minuteman,"[lxxxi] and would put a brake on the development of highly-accurate, counter-silo ICBMs by the superpowers.

The Soviets, however, had a different view of the proposal. The SS-18 was a keystone in their strategic forces, representing an enormous investment in time and resources over the past several years. To ask that this force be halved in return for a promise to not deploy a weapon that was still in the developmental stage—and was, even without a SALT II agreement, many years away from deployment—was simply unacceptable to Moscow. This effort was seen as upsetting the very delicate nature of the SALT negotiations, as the level of 308 had been agreed to at Vladivostok, which the Soviets believed would be the basis for negotiation of any SALT II treaty. In the end, the "Comprehensive Proposal" only harmed U.S.-Soviet relations, by making it seem that the Carter Administration would aim for radical proposals severely limiting Soviet strategic arms, while leaving their American equivalents largely unaffected.[lxxxii]

These Soviet concerns were soon apparent to the Americans. A CIA study of Soviet perceptions toward SALT negotiations, presented to President Carter in June 1977, made several two key observations at the outset regarding Soviet positions on this issue. "The strong Soviet resistance to interference with their ongoing strategic programs makes any but token reductions in force levels in SALT II unlikely." More specifically, "The Soviets are unlikely to agree to substantial reductions in heavy ICBMs in SALT II, although they might accept a token cut."[lxxxiii] Under the heading of heavy ICBMs, the report noted:

"The SS-18 heavy ICBM is seen by the Soviets as the key system for implementing a counterforce strategy. These missiles probably are regarded highly both for their ability to destroy hardened targets and for their political value…the Soviet position remains that the issue was settled in the first Interim Agreement of 1972 and at Vladivostok, and that further limitations on heavy ICBMs are unacceptable. The Soviets probably will remain wedded to this position with the possible exception of some token alterations in response to other US concessions."[lxxxiv]

Given these perceptions, based heavily on past Soviet behavior and particularly on the experience of March 1977, the Carter Administration, with an eye to both strategic and domestic factors in arms control, began to move toward the development of MX as a means of rectifying U.S. ICBM vulnerability.

In his memoirs, Brzezinski noted that "Both Harold Brown and I felt strongly that the United States would be at a strategic disadvantage if SALT II was not accompanied by new strategic deployments by the U.S. side."[lxxxv] Continuing on this point, Brzezinski specified the system needed to restore stability to the balance. "Given the growing accuracy and numbers of Soviet land-based missiles, the existing American land-based deterrent was becoming increasingly vulnerable, and it urgently needed modernization.

That modernization required larger, more accurate, and less vulnerable ICBMs than the existing Minuteman III force."[lxxxvi] President Carter, who had had reservations regarding the MX, had continually asked Harold Brown whether the United States could not make do with a dyad of cruise missile-equipped bombers and ballistic missile submarines rather than the existing triad including ICBM. Brown convinced Carter that the triad was necessary in order to maintain a stable strategic balance.[lxxxvii]

At a meeting of the National Security Council on June 4, 1979, Brzezinski, in his opening statement on the U.S.-Soviet military balance, pointed out the adverse trends that increasingly favored the Soviet Union. He warned that, in the early-1980s, the United States "would face a 'strategic dip.' We would not meet the criteria established in Presidential Directive 18; namely, to maintain essential equivalence and a balance no worse than that existing in 1977."[lxxxviii] Brzezinski was supported in this assertion by Harold Brown, Secretary of State Cyrus Vance, CIA Director Admiral Stansfield Turner, and General Jones. By the end of the meeting, Carter began to support approval of MX deployment.[lxxxix]

Two days later, with Carter's approval, Brzezinski outlined the decision to deploy MX. Three criteria were outlined: it would be verifiable under SALT provisions, and would probably utilize a mobile ground shelter system; it would be the largest possible ICBM allowed under SALT II; and, within several weeks of the conclusion of SALT II, the deployment mode would be agreed upon.[xc]

In the final SALT II agreement, provisions for a mobile, MIRVed ICBM were made. Article IV, Paragraph 9 stated that "Each party undertakes not to flight-test or deploy new types of ICBMs, that is, types of ICBMs not flight-tested as of May 1, 1979, *except that each party may flight-test and deploy one new type of light ICBM*" (My italics).[xci] Under treaty provisions, a light ICBM, somewhat ambiguously, was considered in the context of the definition of a heavy ICBM. Article II, Paragraph 7 defined this as:

> "Heavy ICBMs are ICBMs which have a launch-weight greater than that of the heavies, in terms of either launch-weight or throw-weight, respectively, of the light ICBMs deployed by either party as of the date of signature of this Treaty."[xcii]

The MX had a throwweight of 7,900lb, together with a payload of 7,200lb. Its weight at launch was 193,000lb.[xciii] Given that these figures approached those of the Soviet SS-19 ICBM, the threshold for what was considered a "light" ICBM was set quite high!

Article IV, Paragraph 11 established that these "light" ICBMs could be tested with a maximum of 10 MIRVs, which was what was planned for the MX.[xciv] The only real

limitations, spelled out in Article IX, was a ban on *heavy* mobile ICBM, as well as on deployment of mobile ICBMs on the seabed "or on the beds of internal waters and inland waters."[xcv] This translated into a minor restriction on deployment of the MX, and prohibited the Soviet Union from deploying the SS-18, its heavy ICBM, in a similar fashion. Thus, SALT II was able to incorporate an important element of U.S. strategic force planning, which itself was shaped by the debate over land-based ICBM forces.

What SALT II was unable to curb, however, was improved ICBM accuracy.

The MX was meant to be a highly accurate, counterforce missile with prompt hard-target kill capability. Had there been accuracy limitations, this would have undermined the rationale for the MX, since the viability of the ICBM leg of the triad was in question. Part of this viability was the need to maintain flexible options in the event of a strategic nuclear conflict. This meant, of course, that the Soviets could also deploy a mobile ICBM with 10 MIRVs, and that the accuracy of such missiles as the SS-17, SS-18 and SS-19 could be improved. The compromise on mobile ICBMs allowed the United States to go forward with a solution to its vulnerability dilemma but, ironically, exacerbated it as well.[xcvi]

Conclusion.

The debate regarding ICBM vulnerability, and its implications for the U.S. strategic deterrent, played a significant role in influencing the outcome of the SALT II debate during 1979. Public opinion polls during this time show just how Americans viewed the apparently shifting strategic balance, and the impact that this debate had in shaping that view. A poll conducted in February and March 1979 by the CPD is telling in this regard. Its pollsters asked respondents carefully worded questions regarding aspects of the military balance and SALT II. Among the questions asked was whether or not respondents would support SALT II with the knowledge that, by the year of its expiry (1985), "the ability of Soviet ballistic missiles to destroy American missile sites and other protected military targets is expected to be ten times that of U.S. ballistic missiles' ability to destroy similar targets in Russia."

Put this way, 26.5 per cent of respondents were "much more inclined to *oppose* the treaty" while another 21.1 per cent were "somewhat more inclined to *oppose* the treaty."[xcvii] The total was thus 47.6 per cent in opposition to SALT II on these grounds. Taken together, this meant that opponents were the largest group in the survey response to this question, an indication of how the perceived vulnerability of U.S. ICBMs had helped to shape public opinion.[xcviii]

Although the poll by the CPD did tend to lead to answers showing opposition to SALT II, it is a good example of how the hawks were able to shape and mobilize public opinion against the Treaty, based on issues of American vulnerability to Soviet strategic forces. Prominent hawks like Gray, Nitze and Pipes were able to use the pages of widely read journals like *Foreign Affairs*, *Foreign Policy* and *Commentary* to get their message out to the American public. Most of the publications favored by the doves, like the *Defense Monitor*, were not nearly as widely disseminated. Furthermore, the CPD and other groups opposed to SALT II for similar reasons engaged in successful fund-raising campaigns to support their cause. This meant that more money was available to produce publications and films like *First Strike*[xcix] regarding the vulnerability issue. Compared to the doves, the hawks (according to the *Christian Science Monitor*) spent 15 times more in getting public support against SALT II than the doves.[c]

Perhaps most important was that the hawks, led by the CPD, had a clear position on the vulnerability issue (and therefore opposition to SALT II). The doves tended to be divided over SALT II, since some saw it as merely cosmetic arms control and not nearly as far-reaching as it should have been.[ci] Moreover, the specific issue of vulnerability was not refuted with the same vigor that the hawks had advocated it, particularly at the grass roots level. Doves preferred to sidestep the issue, believing that the U.S. ICBM force would become vulnerable with or without SALT II. While admitting to the vulnerability factor, they believed that it was bearable. "It should be possible for the U.S. to learn to live with realistic projections of ICBM survivability," the *Defense Monitor* reported in 1977 "as we have learned to live with the vulnerability of cities."[cii] This was in marked contrast to the strident view of the hawks on this issue, and their very public stance. Similarly, whereas the hawks had demanded a SALT agreement that called for major reductions, including those on the SS-18 and SS-19 ICBMs, the doves, as a group, tended to see SALT II, with all its flaws, as being in the mold of "something is better than nothing."

At the official level, ICBM vulnerability was affected by such efforts, particularly as they affected the views of the U.S. Senate, which would have to ratify any SALT II agreement in order for it to become a treaty. Moreover, the unwillingness of the Soviets to negotiate on the issue of heavy ICBM levels meant that the only apparent remedy to this state of affairs was the development and deployment of a survivable ICBM, namely the MX.

Finally, the issue of ICBM vulnerability, as part of the overall debate about the superpower military balance, reflected the growing concern among Americans that the United States, on the whole, was vulnerable to an ever more powerful Soviet Union.

The events of this period—the Soviet role in the Horn of Africa during 1977-78, the "crisis" over the Soviet brigade in Cuba in 1979 and the Soviet invasion of Afghanistan at the end of that year—were seen as an indication of Moscow's ability to use its military strength to establish itself in areas of vital interest to the United States (i.e. in proximity to the Persian Gulf and in the Caribbean.)

This, in turn, led back to the hawks' argument that Soviet strategic power provided a bedrock for such actions, just as Nitze and others had warned. Their view of Soviet strategic capabilities had shaped perceptions, both at the elite and popular levels, that such capabilities had led to a more aggressive and dangerous Soviet mode of behavior in international relations. According to this view, the apparent vulnerability of the U.S. strategic deterrent, particularly the ICBM force, was the most important indicator of an unwillingness on the part of the United States to confront this new reality.

With the onset of the Second Cold War by 1980, and the coming to office of Ronald Reagan the following year (whose national security bureaucracy included many members of the CPD like Gray, Nitze and Pipes in important positions), these arguments would come to shape important policy areas like strategic forces development and arms control in the 1980s. Thus would a technological issue come to play an important (and unforeseen) role in shaping U.S. domestic politics and international relations.

---

[i] John M. Collins, *American and Soviet Military Trends Since the Cuban Missile Crisis* (Washington, D.C.: Center for Strategic and International Studies, Georgetown University, 1978), pp. 92, 97, 98. The specific numbers for 1970 were 1,427 ICBMs and 289 SLBMs (deployed on 40 ballistic missile submarines), while the numbers for 1977 were 1,469 ICBMs and 878 SLBMs (on 86 submarines.)

[ii] MIRVs are warheads that can be programmed to strike different targets. Multiple re-entry vehicles (MRV) can only strike one target, in a manner similar to a shotgun shell.

[iii] Norman Polmar, *Strategic Weapons: An Introduction* (London: Macdonald & Jane's, Limited, 1976), p. ix.

[iv] In establishing the categories of "hawks" and "doves," it is important to note that these labels do not translate into common political or even overall strategic views among their members. Among the "doves," for instance, was Jan Lodal, a member of the National Security Council during the Ford Administration, whose political views differed considerably from those of Admiral Gene LaRoque, USN (Ret.), founder of the Center for Defense Information (CDI), or of writer Andrew Cockburn. In this context, "hawks" refers to those who believed that ICBM vulnerability could be rectified mainly through military means (i.e. deployment of new weaponry like mobile ICBMs), and "doves" to those who believed that such vulnerability was not an issue of great importance in the overall strategic balance.

[v] Ray Bonds, Ed. *The Soviet War Machine: An Encyclopedia of Russian Military Equipment and Strategy* (London: Salamander Books, 1976), p. 212 on MIRV capabilities and International Institute for Strategic Studies (IISS*) Strategic Survey 1980-1981* (London: IISS, 1981), p. 13 on accuracy.

[vi] Paul H. Nitze, "Assuring Strategic Stability in an Era of Détente," *Foreign Affairs*, Vol. 54, No. 2 (January 1976), p. 226.

[vii] Nitze, "Deterring our Deterrent," *Foreign Policy*, No. 25 (Winter 1976-77), p. 208.

[viii] Charles Tyroler II, *Alerting America: The Papers of the Committee on the Present Danger* (McLean, VA: Pergamon-Brassey's International Defense Publishers, 1984), pp. 49-50.

[ix] Additionally, Collins points out the location of the Soviet core areas, which he defines as "geographically distinct aggregations of great political, economic, and/or cultural significance, the seizure, retention, destruction, or control of which would afford marked advantage to any opponent." (John M. Collins, *U.S.-Soviet Military Balance: Concepts and Capabilities 1960-1980* [New York, NY: McGraw-Hill Publications, 1980], p. 130). Of nine such areas, only two, at Leningrad and Vladivostok, were along the coast. Given that the Poseidon C-3 SLBM's range was 2,500 nautical miles, this meant that "Four of the five crucial centers in European Russia lie several hundred miles or more behind air defense shields, and make present generation U.S. SLBMs stretch from most launch points." (Ibid.).

[x] Richard Pipes, *U.S.-Soviet Relations in the Era of Détente* (Boulder, CO: Westview Press, Inc., 1981), pp. 155-156.

[xi] Anne Hessing Cahn, *Killing Détente: the Right Attacks the CIA* (College Park, PA: The Pennsylvania State University Press, 1998), p. 139.

[xii] "Intelligence Community Experiment in Competitive Analysis: Soviet Strategic Objectives: An Alternative View; Report of Team 'B,'" (December 1976), p. 21.

[xiii] Ibid.

[xiv] David H. Dunn, *The Politics of Threat: Minuteman Vulnerability in American National Security Policy* (London: Macmillan Press, Ltd., 1997), p. 110.

[xv] IISS *Strategic Survey 1980-1981*, (London: IISS, 1981), p. 13.

[xvi] Colin S. Gray, "The Strategic Forces Triad: End of the Road?" *Foreign Affairs* Vol. 56, No. 4 (July 1978), p. 774.

[xvii] Gray, p. 783.

[xviii] Gray, p. 788.

[xix] Thomas B. Cochran, William M. Arkin and Milton M. Hoenig, *Nuclear Weapons Databook: Volume 1 U.S. Nuclear Forces and Capabilities* (Cambridge, MA: Ballinger Publishing Company, 1983), p. 120.

[xx] Colin S. Gray, *The MX ICBM and National Security* (New York, NY: Praeger Publishers, 1981), p. 40.

[xxi] George B. Kistiakowsky, "The Arms Race: Is Paranoia Necessary for Security?" *The Defense Monitor*, Vol. VII, No. 3 (March 1978), p. 6.

[xxii] Ibid.

[xxiii] Andrew Cockburn, *The Threat: Inside the Soviet Military Machine* (New York, NY: Vintage Books, 1983), pp. 309-310.

[xxiv] Cockburn, p. 310.

[xxv] "The Obsolete ICBM," *The Defense Monitor*, Vol. VIII, No. 4 (March 1979), p. 7.

[xxvi] "The Obsolete ICBM," p. 6.

[xxvii] Jan M. Lodal, "Assuring Strategic Stability: An Alternative View," *Foreign Affairs*, Vol. 54, No.3 (April 1976), p. 467.

[xxviii] Cockburn, p. 308.

[xxix] Christopher Coker, *US Military Power in the 1980s* (London and Basingstoke: The Macmillan Press, Ltd., 1983), p. 55.

[xxx] Lodal, p. 465.

[xxxi] John .M. Collins and Anthony Cordesman, *Imbalance of Power: Shifting U.S.-Soviet Military Strengths* (San Rafael, CA: Presidio Press, 1978), p. 49.

[xxxii] "The Obsolete ICBM," pp. 2-3.

[xxxiii] See *The Defense Monitor*, Volume VI, No. 6 (August 1977) and Volume VIII, No. 9 (October 1979) for a detailed discussion of these factors.

[xxxiv] *Report of the Secretary of Defense Donald H. Rumsfeld to the Congress on the FY 1977 Budget and its Implications for the FY 1978 Authorization Request and the FY 1977-1981 Defense Programs* (Washington, D.C.: United States Government Printing Office (USGPO), January 27, 1976), pp. 52-53. Henceforth *Report FY 1977*.

[xxxv] *Report of Secretary of Defense Donald H. Rumsfeld to the Congress on the FY 1978 Budget, FY 1979 Authorization Request and FY 1978-1982 Defense Programs* (Washington, D.C.: USGPO, January 17, 1977), p. 19 (Executive Summary). Henceforth *Report FY 1978*.

[xxxvi] Donald Rumsfeld, Secretary of Defense. *U.S. Defense Perspectives Fiscal Year 1978* (Washington, D.C.: USGPO, January 1977), p. 19. Henceforth *Defense 1978*.

[xxxvii] *Report FY 1977*, p. iv.

[xxxviii] Ibid.

[xxxix] *Department of Defense Annual Report Fiscal Year 1979: Harold Brown, Secretary of Defense*, (Washington, D.C.: USGPO, February 2, 1978), p. 63. Henceforth *Report FY 1979.*

[xl] *Report FY 1979*, pp. 63-64. These points were made at the beginning of the Carter Administration in testimony before the Senate Foreign Relations Committee. Sidney D. Drell, the deputy director of Stanford University's Linear Accelerator Center, stated that the United States enjoyed a superiority in MIRVed warheads "and is pursuing highly sophisticated accuracy programs" for its forces. Drell then noted the impact such programs might have in Moscow. "Thus it is not without cause…that the Soviet Union…shows concern with our programs similar to our concern with theirs." (M. Marder, "Experts Clash on Nuclear Arms Balance," *The Washington Post*, 20 January, 1977, p. A20.)

[xli] *Report FY 1979*, p. 64.

[xlii] *Report of Secretary of Defense Harold Brown to the Congress on the FY 1980 Budget, FY 1981 Authorization Request and FY 1980-1984 Defense Programs* (Washington, D.C.: USGPO, January 25, 1979), p. 81. Henceforth *Report FY 1980.*

[xliii] *Report FY 1980*, p. 79.

[xliv] *Report of Secretary of Defense Harold Brown to the Congress on the FY 1981 Budget, FY 1982 Authorization Request and FY 1981-1985 Defense Programs* (Washington, D.C.: USGPO, January 29, 1980), p. 127. Henceforth *Report FY 1981.*

[xlv] *Report FY 1981*, p. 128. See also R. Burt, "Brown Says ICBM's May Be Vulnerable To The Russians Now," *The New York Times*, 21 August 1980, p. A2.

[xlvi] *Report of Secretary of Defense Harold Brown to the Congress on the FY 1982 Budget, FY 1983 Authorization Request and FY 1982-1986 Defense Programs* (Washington, D.C.: USGPO, January 19, 1981), p. 111. Henceforth *Report FY 1982.*

[xlvii] *Fiscal Year 1978 Authorization for Military Procurement, Research and Development, and Active Duty, Selected Reserve, and Civilian Personnel Strengths, Hearings Before the Committee on Armed Services United States Senate, 95th Congress* (Washington, D.C.: USGPO, March 17, 1977), p. 6054. Henceforth *Hearings.*

[xlviii] *Hearings*, p. 6055.

[xlix] Polmar, op. cit., p. 111.

[l] Polmar, op. cit., p. 117.

[li] *Statement by General George S. Brown, USAF Chairman, Joint Chiefs of staff to the Congress on the Defense Posture of the United States for FY 1977* (Washington, D.C.: USGPO, 20 January 1976), p. 32. Henceforth *Posture FY 1977.*

[lii] *Posture FY 1977*, p. 49.

[liii] Ibid.

[liv] Ibid.

[lv] *Statement by General George S. Brown, USAF Chairman, Joint Chiefs of Staff to the Congress on the Defense Posture of the United States for FY_1978* (Washington, D.C.: USGPO, 20 January 1977), p. 12.

[lvi] Ibid.

[lvii] *Statement by General George S. Brown, USAF Chairman, Joint Chiefs of Staff to the Congress on the Defense Posture of the United States for FY 1979* (Washington, D.C.: USGPO, 20 January 1978), p. 8. Henceforth *Posture FY 1979.*

[lviii] *Posture FY 1979*, p. 22.

[lix] *United States Military Posture for FY 1980: An Overview by General David C. Jones, USAF Chairman of the Joint Chiefs of Staff* (Washington, D.C.: USGPO, 1979), p. vi. Henceforth *Posture FY 1980.*

[lx] Ibid.

[lxi] *Posture FY 1980*, p. 7.

[lxii] *Posture FY 1980*, P. 27.

[lxiii] *United States Military Posture for FY 1981: An Overview by General David C. Jones, USAF Chairman of the Joint Chiefs of Staff* (Washington, D.C.: USGPO, January 29, 1980), p. iii. Henceforth *Posture FY 1981.*

[lxiv] *Posture FY 1981*, p. 12.

[lxv] *United States Military Posture: An Overview by General David C. Jones, USAF Chairman of the Joint Chiefs of Staff for FY 1982* (Washington, D.C.: USGPO, 1981), p. iv. Henceforth *Posture FY 1982.*

[lxvi] *Posture FY 1982*, p. 1.

[lxvii] *Posture FY 1982*, p. 23.

[lxviii] Memo, Senator Henry M. Jackson to Jimmy Carter, "Memorandum for the President on SALT," 15 February 1977, in USSR/US Conference 5/94 Briefing Book (II), Box 117, Vertical File, Jimmy Carter Library.

[lxix] Ibid.

[lxx] Ibid.

[lxxi] *Land-Based ICBM Forces Vulnerability and Options*, Intelligence and Military Application of Nuclear Energy Subcommittee of the Committee on Armed Services, House of Representatives, 95th Congress 2nd Session (Washington, D.C.: USGPO, October 5, 1978), p. 1. Henceforth *ICBM Forces.*

[lxxii] Ibid.

[lxxiii] *ICBM Forces*, pp. 2-3.

[lxxiv] *ICBM Forces*, p. 14.

[lxxv] Cochran, Arkin and Hoenig, p. 122.

[lxxvi] National Security Council Meeting Minutes, "SALT (and Angola)," 22 December 1975, Box 2 National Security Adviser, National Security Council Meetings File, Gerald R. Ford Library.

[lxxvii] This was the term used to describe the Vladivostok Accord (In Dan Caldwell, *The Dynamics of Domestic Politics and Arms Control: The SALT II Treaty Ratification Debate* (Columbia, SC: University of South Carolina Press, 1991), p. 36.)

[lxxviii] "Aide Memoire, Henry Kissinger to Anatoly Dobrynin," 10 December 1974, USSR/US Conference 5/94 Briefing Book (II), Box 117, Vertical File, Jimmy Carter Library.

[lxxix] "Memorandum of Conversation, The President, Anatoliy Dobrynin, et.al.," 1 February 1977, USSR Related Documents Opened (I), Box 116, Vertical File, Jimmy Carter Library.

[lxxx] Memo, Zbigniew Brzezinski to Jimmy Carter, "Summary Report for your Information and Reaction of the Special Coordination Committee Meeting, Feb. 3," 3 February 1977, USSR 1980-1995, Box 116, Vertical File, Jimmy Carter Library.

[lxxxi] Dunn, p. 103.

[lxxxii] This would have an unfortunate effect on efforts to rally American public and Congressional support for SALT II. As Dunn points out, "The CP [Comprehensive Proposal] had set an impossible standard for the administration while at the same time giving ground to its critics in its apparent acceptance that the threat to Minuteman was something which it was vital for SALT to address. The real position, namely that Carter saw the need to address ICBM vulnerability as a domestic political issue rather than an external strategic problem, was a subtlety lost in the debate" (p. 104.)

[lxxxiii] Memo, Stanfield Turner to Jimmy Carter, "An Assessment of Soviet Perceptions on SALT-May 1977," 2 June 1977, USSR Related Documents Opened (I), Box 116, Vertical File, Jimmy Carter Library.

[lxxxiv] Ibid.

[lxxxv] Zbigniew Brzezinski, *Power and Principle: Memoirs of the National Security Adviser 1977-1981* (New York, NY: Farrar-Straus-Giroux, 1983), p. 332.

[lxxxvi] Ibid.

[lxxxvii] Brzezinski, p. 334.

[lxxxviii] Brzezinski, p. 335.

[lxxxix] Brzezinski, p. 335-336.

[xc] Brzezinski, p. 336.

[xci] "The SALT II Treaty," *Survival*, Vol. XXI, No. 5 (September/October 1979), p. 218.

[xcii] Ibid.

[xciii] Cochran, Arkin and Hoenig, p. 121.

[xciv] *Survival* (September/October 1979), p. 218.

[xcv] *Survival* (September/October 1979), p. 220.

[xcvi] According to Desmond Ball, the U.S. Air Force, which would deploy the MX, had made its decision on the MX's characteristics some time before 1979. "The USAF had long decided what sort of a follow-on ICBM it wanted...Counterforce came before more survivability, regardless of the requirements of the other elements of U.S. strategic nuclear policy," in *Developments in U.S. Strategic Nuclear Policy Under the Carter Administration* (Los Angeles, CA: ACIS Working Paper No. 21, Center for International and Strategic Affairs, University of California, Los Angeles, February 1980), p. 15.

[xcvii] Tyroler, p. 121.

[xcviii] Ibid.

[xcix] This film, first shown in 1980 on San Francisco public television, provides a good summary of the hawks' case regarding the issue of ICBM vulnerability. The film posits a hypothetical scenario involving a Soviet counterforce strike on the U.S. strategic forces. According to the filmmakers, just 34 minutes after a Soviet first strike (in which eight million Americans have died), only 46 Minuteman ICBMs (out of 1,000 deployed) remain operational; all but 22 of 330 B-52 bombers have been destroyed, while 17 of 41 ballistic missile submarines have been lost in port, with more at sea. The U.S. President, faced with the certainty of a Soviet countervalue strike if he orders retaliation, instead directs surviving U.S. forces to cease fire, just nine minutes after the attack. The film then continues with commentary on the strategic balance, including the importance of ICBMs, the secondary role of bombers and submarines in counterforce strategies, and interviews with experts, including William Van Cleave, Edward Luttwak and James Schlesinger. It also includes a segment with Paul Nitze, who explains the dangers of an effective Soviet counterforce strategy as linked to Soviet geopolitical objectives. According to Nitze, these include the neutralization of NATO Europe, the People's Republic of China and Japan, and, most importantly, control of the Persian Gulf, since Moscow's ability to dictate the flow of energy supplies would allow for Soviet global dominance. To Nitze, the Gulf was a fulcrum for the superpowers' foreign policies. *First Strike* (San Francisco, CA: KRON-TV Documentary Unit Production, Chronicle Broadcasting Co., 1980.)

[c] Dunn, p. 97.

[ci] Dunn, pp. 96-97.

[cii] "The $100 Million Mobile Missile: The MX and the Future of U.S. Strategic Forces," *The Defense Monitor*, Vol. VI, No. 6 (August 1977), p. 8.

15179389R10026

Printed in Great Britain
by Amazon